OKLAHOMA

JEOPARDY!

Answers and Questions About Our State

by
Carole Marsh

I0867737

This activity book has material which correlates with Oklahoma's Priority Academic Student Skills. At every opportunity, we have tried to relate information to the History and Social Science, English, Science, Math, Civics, Economics, and Computer Technology PASS directives. For additional information, go to our websites: **www.oklahomaexperience.com** or **www.gallopade.com**.

Correlates with Oklahoma's PASS Priority Academic Student Skills

GALLOPADE INTERNATIONAL

Reading Research Reinforcement Reference

Gallopade is proud to be a member of these educational organizations and associations:

SHOPA MEMBER™ School, Home, & Office Products Association

NSSEA

ASCD

The Oklahoma Experience Series

The Oklahoma Experience! Paperback Book

My First Pocket Guide to Oklahoma!

The Big Oklahoma Reproducible Activity Book

The Oklahoma Coloring Book!

My First Book About Oklahoma!

Oklahoma Jeopardy: Answers and Questions About Our State

Oklahoma Jography: A Fun Run Through Our State

The Oklahoma Experience! Sticker Pack

The Oklahoma Experience! Poster/Map

Discover Oklahoma CD-ROM

Oklahoma "GEO" Bingo Game

Oklahoma "HISTO" Bingo Game

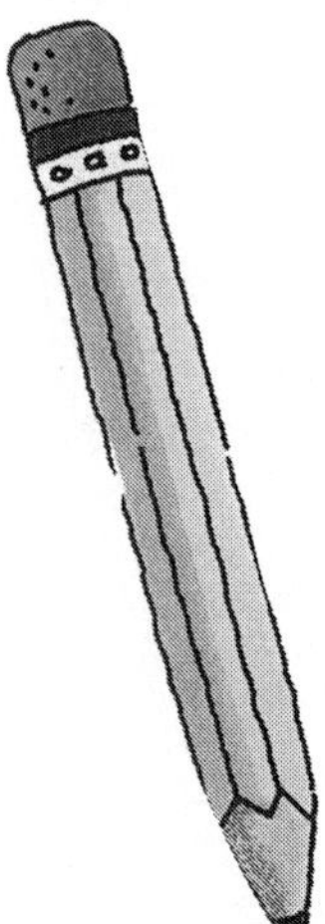

A Word... from the Author

The word is Jeopardy!

I'm sure you've all seen this popular game show. Actually, it's not much different from something kids seem to hate—the good, old-fashioned pop quiz! But how much more fun plain, boring questions and answers are when they're switcherooed into answers and questions!

I'm not trying to copy the actual Jeopardy game show format. I've just tried to use the reverse: "Here's the answer, now what's the question?" formula to make the facts about our state as interesting and intriguing as possible. Also, I think this format is a good double-check to see just how much all that history and geography is registering. Kids often know "facts" only in the memorized-order they learned them, which does not exactly = true knowledge, even if they do pass their tests.

The Answers and Questions on the next pages cover our state's history, geography, people, and much more. You can use the book in a variety of ways. If students want to read it on their own, they'll need to use a sheet of paper to cover the answers, oops!, I mean the questions. You could keep the book on the kitchen table and play Jeopardy while you eat breakfast. In the classroom, you could give the answers orally and let kids give the questions.

Whatever you do, keep score, have fun, let all ages participate, use wrong answers (I mean questions!) as the starting point for improved learning. Let kids have a chance to create their own Jeopardy answers and questions (it's much harder than it looks!). The only thing that should really be put in jeopardy are your frown muscles!

Carole Marsh

Oklahoma Trivia

Answer: The state capital of Oklahoma

QUESTION: What is Oklahoma City?

Answer: Oklahoma's state motto

QUESTION: What is "Labor Conquers All Things"?

Answer: Town known as the "Trout Capital of Oklahoma"

QUESTION: What is Gore?

Answer: The state soil

QUESTION: What is Port Silt Loam?

Answer: Oklahoma's state song

QUESTION: What is "Oklahoma"?

Oklahoma

All Around Our State

Answer: The river that determines Oklahoma's southern border

QUESTION: What is the Red River?

Answer: States that form Oklahoma's eastern border

QUESTION: What are Arkansas and Missouri?

Answer: The highest point in Oklahoma

QUESTION: What is Black Mesa?

Answer: Oklahoma's northern border states

QUESTION: What are Kansas and Colorado?

Answer: Oklahoma's southern border state

QUESTION: What is Texas?

Oklahoma

This Land is Our Land

Answer: Military post that is home to the U.S. Army Field Artillery Center and School

QUESTION: What is Fort Sill?

Answer: The fort established by Major Stephen Long on the Arkansas River in 1817

QUESTION: What is Fort Smith?

Answer: Custer's headquarters during his battles with the Plains Indians

QUESTION: What is Fort Supply?

Answer: Forts built in 1824 in northeast and southeast Oklahoma to protect settlers from the Spanish and the Indians

QUESTION: What are Forts Gibson and Towson?

Answer: A military park where both U.S. President Zachary Taylor and Confederate President Jefferson Davis served

QUESTION: What is Fort Gibson?

Oklahoma Early Days

Answer: Scholars believe that the inscription on this indicates Norsemen may have come to Oklahoma as early as 1012.

QUESTION: What is the Heavener Runestone?

Answer: Historical site that has 12 earthen mounds and the remains of a village

QUESTION: What are the Spiro Mounds?

Answer: Explorer who claimed the western half of the Mississippi River Valley for Spain in 1541 and crossed the Oklahoma Panhandle

QUESTION: Who was Francisco Vásquez de Coronado?

Answer: Spanish explorer who explored eastern Oklahoma

QUESTION: Who was Hernando De Soto?

Answer: He claimed all of the land drained by the western tributaries of the Mississippi River for France in 1682.

QUESTION: Who was René-Robert Cavelier, Sieur de La Salle?

Oklahoma

Patriotic People

Answer: She started Boley, the largest predominantly African-American town in the west, on the 80 acres of land she owned.

QUESTION: Who was Abigail Barnett?

Answer: Oklahoma congressman who served as speaker of the house from 1970–1976

QUESTION: Who was Carl Albert?

Answer: He became the first elected chief of the Cherokees in 1971, the first to be elected since Oklahoma became a state.

QUESTION: Who was William "Bill" Keeler?

Answer: The first of Oklahoma's governors to be born in the state

QUESTION: Who was Robert Samuel Kerr?

Answer: She is known as the "first lady of Oklahoma history."

QUESTION: Who is Angie Debo?

Oklahoma Conflicts and Hostilities

Answer: Secret network that helped escaped slaves get to the North

QUESTION: What was the Underground Railroad?

Answer: He was a Native American Confederate general whose troops captured 300 Union supply wagons at the Battle of Cabin Creek.

QUESTION: Who was Stand Watie?

Answer: Black and white soldiers fought together for the first time during this Civil War battle near present-day Muskogee.

QUESTION: What was the Battle of Honey Springs?

Answer: The leaders of this Indian group committed their people to the Confederate cause during the Civil War.

QUESTION: Who were the Five Civilized Tribes?

Answer: The site where Confederate troops attacked nearly 5,000 Creek Union loyalists headed for Kansas on November 19, 1861

QUESTION: What is Round Mountain?

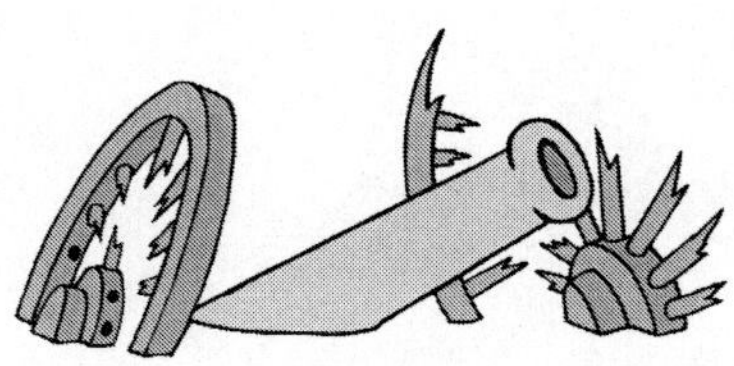

Oklahoma Real Estate

Answer: Memorials to Will Rogers and Lynn Riggs are found here.

QUESTION: What is Claremore?

Answer: This is the town where the Trail of Tears ended and the three branches of the Cherokee tribe formed the Cherokee Nation.

QUESTION: What is Tahlequah?

Answer: Home of the University of Oklahoma

QUESTION: What is Norman?

Answer: City that is home to the Mansion of Mattie Beal

QUESTION: What is Lawton?

Answer: Location of Indian City U.S.A., seven authentically reconstructed Plains Indian villages

QUESTION: What is Anadarko?

Oklahoma

A Date To Remember

Monday	Tuesday	Wednesday	Thursday	Friday	Saturday	Sunday
		1	2	3	4	5

Answer: In 1803, this country bought the Louisiana Territory from France for $15 million.

QUESTION: What is the United States?

Answer: President who opened up two million acres (800,000 hectares) of land to homesteaders starting at noon on April 22, 1889

QUESTION: Who was Benjamin Harrison?

Answer: Oklahoma's first newspaper was published in 1844 in both Cherokee and English.

QUESTION: What is the *Cherokee Advocate?*

Answer: Forced march that took place during the winter of 1838–39 when U.S. soldiers rounded up the Five Civilized Tribes and took them to Oklahoma

QUESTION: What was the Trail of Tears?

Answer: During the winter of 1868, this Cheyenne chief and more than 100 of his people were killed when attacked by soldiers led by Lieutenant Colonel George Armstrong Custer.

QUESTION: Who was Black Kettle?

Oklahoma

Scholarly Smarts

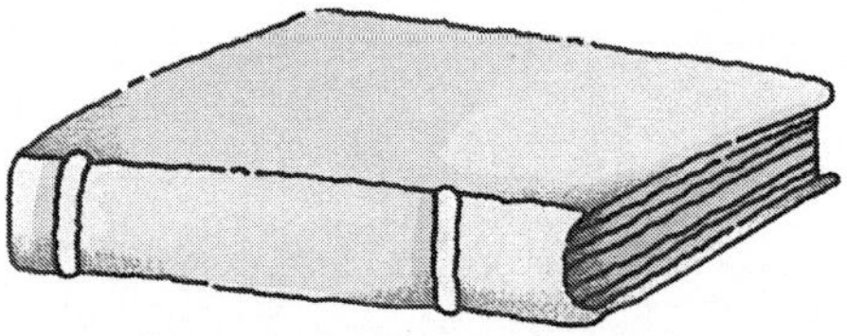

Answer: They started the first schools in Oklahoma and modeled them after schools in the east.

QUESTION: Who were Native Americans?

Answer: School attendance is required for children ages five to to this age in Oklahoma.

QUESTION: What is 18?

Answer: Satellite and fiber-optic programs that allow rural schools to have access to information and classes at urban schools

QUESTION: What are distance-learning technologies?

Answer: Since 1990, this curriculum has required students be tested at regular intervals on specific subjects.

QUESTION: What is the Priority Academic Student Skills (PASS)?

Answer: The university in Edmond established as a teacher training college in 1890

QUESTION: What is the University of Central Oklahoma?

Oklahoma

First and Foremost

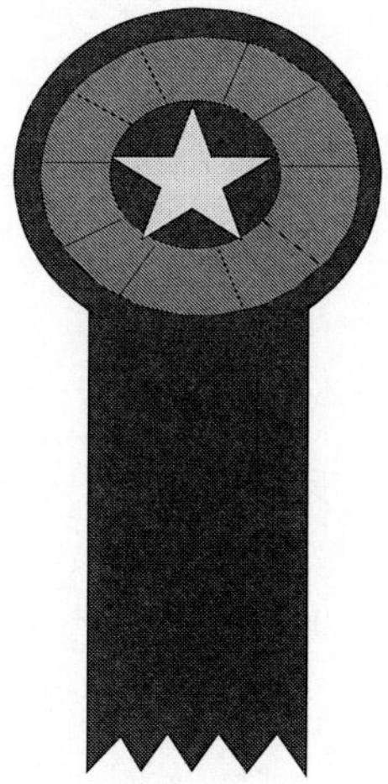

Answer: He drilled the first commercial oil in the state in 1897 and went on to establish Phillips Petroleum Company.

QUESTION: Who was Frank Phillips?

Answer: The Glenpool oil field was discovered under his land in 1905 and by the age of 27, he had 32 wells producing oil on his land.

QUESTION: Who was Thomas Gilcrease?

Answer: The oil prospector who drilled the state's first oil-producing well near Chelsea in 1889

QUESTION: Who was Edward Byrd?

Answer: Oklahoman who was the first athlete to win the decathlon and pentathlon at the 1912 Olympics

QUESTION: Who was Jim Thorpe?

Answer: Oklahoma's leading cash crop and most important export crop

QUESTION: What is wheat?

Oklahoma

Cowboys and Cattle Trails

Answer: The best known cattle trail that went through Oklahoma and was named after a part-Cherokee trader

QUESTION: What is the Chisholm Trail?

Answer: They began as sporting events for cowboys.

QUESTION: What are rodeos?

Answer: After Oklahoma homesteaders did this to their land, uninterrupted cattle drives became difficult.

QUESTION: What is fencing their land?

Answer: The cattle trails led to markets and railyards in this state.

QUESTION: What is Kansas?

Answer: Popular shows that were similar to rodeos, but were more theatrical

QUESTION: What were Wild West Shows?

Oklahoma

Music and Film

Answer: Oklahoma actor known for his roles in *Legends of the Fall* and *A River Runs Through It*

QUESTION: Who is Brad Pitt?

Answer: Oklahoman who stars in the television series *Walker, Texas Ranger*

QUESTION: Who is Chuck Norris?

Answer: Yukon is the hometown of this country music superstar and his alter ego, Chris Gaines.

QUESTION: Who is Garth Brooks?

Answer: World-famous opera star from Enid who originally performed with her 14 brothers and sisters

QUESTION: Who is Leona Mitchell?

Answer: Tulsa-based music group who hit the pop scene in the late 1990s with "MMMBop"

QUESTION: Who is Hanson?

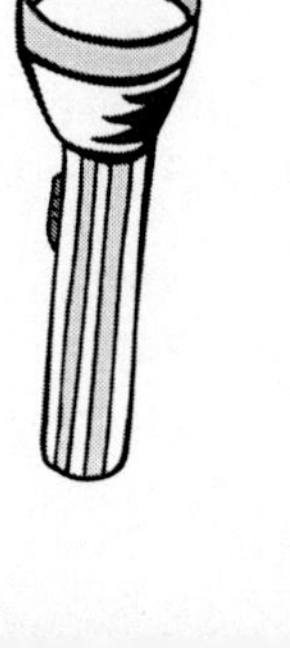

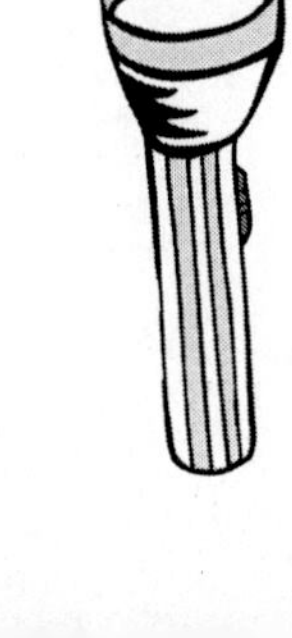

Oklahoma Laudable Landmarks

Answer: Handle-like extension of the state that is 34 miles (54.7 kilometers) wide

QUESTION: What is the Panhandle?

Answer: The grass in this 37,000-acre (14,973-hectare) preserve grows up to 8 feet high (2.44 meters).

QUESTION: What is the Tallgrass Prairie Preserve?

Answer: Lake in east-central Oklahoma that is the state's largest

QUESTION: What is Eufaula Lake?

Answer: The state's two major river systems

QUESTION: What are the Red River and the Arkansas River systems?

Answer: In late October of each year, as many as 10 million crows roost on the tree branches of this area northwest of Anadarko.

QUESTION: What is the Fort Cobb Recreation Area?

Oklahoma Weather or Not

Answer: Violent windstorms that destroy property and can injure or kill people

QUESTION: What is a tornado?

Answer: The average temperature in July

QUESTION: What is 82 degrees Fahrenheit (28 degrees Celsius)?

Answer: The average temperature in January

QUESTION: What is 37 degrees Fahrenheit (3 degrees Celsius)?

Answer: Name given to the years of the great drought that hit the southwest United States, including Oklahoma, in the 1930s

QUESTION: What is the Dust Bowl?

Answer: Oklahoma's average yearly precipitation (rain, snow, and other moisture)

QUESTION: What is 32 inches (81 centimeters)?

Oklahoma Scavenger Hunt

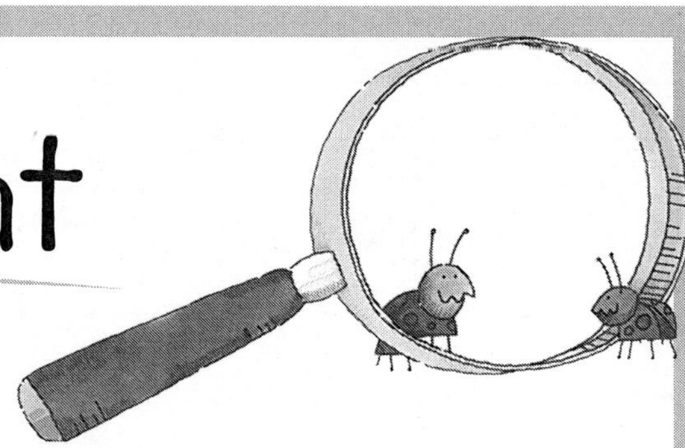

Answer: The nickname given by Indians to the soldiers of the all-black Ninth and Tenth Calvary units stationed at Fort Sill and Fort Gibson

QUESTION: What are Buffalo Soldiers?

Answer: The largest sports arena in Oklahoma that is home to the University of Oklahoma Sooners

QUESTION: What is Oklahoma Memorial Stadium?

Answer: Choctaw County lake that is the largest natural lake in Oklahoma

QUESTION: What is Lake Hugo?

Answer: It is the largest waterfall in the state at a height of 77 feet (23.5 meters).

QUESTION: What is Turner Falls?

Answer: These events brought homesteaders to Oklahoma in the late 1800s and helped spread the population throughout the state.

QUESTION: What were land runs?

Oklahoma Potpourri

Answer: The state animal is a large mammal also known as a bison.

QUESTION: What is an American Buffalo?

Answer: The state bird is a quiet bird named for its deeply forked black-and-white tail.

QUESTION: What is a Scissor-Tailed Flycatcher?

Answer: The state flower

QUESTION: What is Oklahoma Rose?

Answer: The state fish

QUESTION: What is the White or Sand Bass?

Answer: The state grass is also known as Wood Grass.

QUESTION: What is Indian Grass?

Oklahoma

Fairs and Festivals

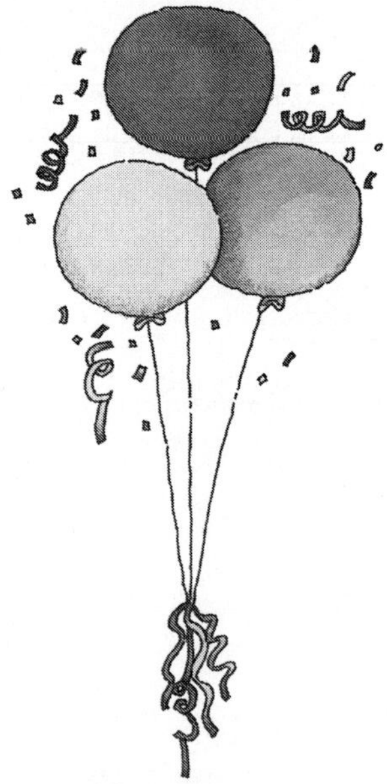

Answer: The third-largest state fair in North America is held in September every year in this city.

QUESTION: What is Oklahoma City?

Answer: The World Championship Hog Calling Contest is held here every February.

QUESTION: What is Weatherford?

Answer: It is held in June each year in Okmulgee and holds the record for the largest pecan pie, cookie, and brownie.

QUESTION: What is the Pecan Festival?

Answer: The country's top performers are among those appearing in concert at the festival held in Hugo in August.

QUESTION: What is the Blue Grass and Old Time Music Festival?

Answer: Indian Nation which hosts an annual homecoming celebration in Tahlequah in September

QUESTION: What is the Cherokee Nation?

Oklahoma

Outlaws and Lawmen

Answer: Name given to Deputy Marshals Bill Tilghman, Heck Thomas, and Chris Madsen

QUESTION: Who were the Three Guardsmen?

Answer: Known as the "Hanging Judge," he was a federal judge who sentenced 172 people to death by hanging.

QUESTION: Who was Issac C. Parker?

Answer: Criminal who kidnapped Oklahoma City oilman Charles F. Urschel and held him for ransom in 1933

QUESTION: Who was Machine-Gun Kelly?

Answer: Outlaw captured by Bill Tilghman who later escaped from a Guthrie prison and was killed in a shootout with a group of lawmen

QUESTION: Who was Bill Doolin?

Answer: The Indian Territory was a favorite hide-out for this woman outlaw.

QUESTION: Who was Belle Starr?

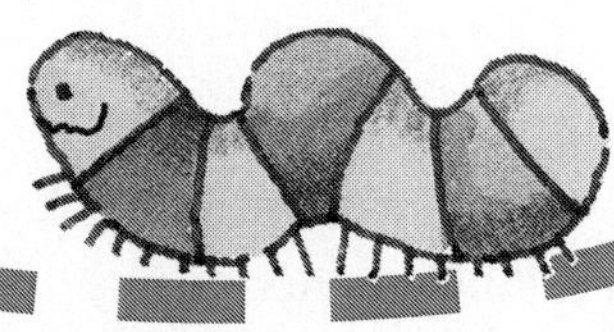

Oklahoma

Powwow

Answer: The name given the five major tribes in the Southeast because many had adopted the customs of Europeans and white Americans

QUESTION: Who were the Five Civilized Tribes?

Answer: The act approved by Congress in 1830 which allowed the government to move the Five Civilized Tribes from the southeast to Oklahoma.

QUESTION: What was the Indian Removal Act?

Answer: The Five Civilized Tribes were forced to sign these after the Civil War and to give up much of the land in the Indian Territory.

QUESTION: What were Reconstruction Treaties?

Answer: A Kiowa leader known as the "Orator of the Plains"

QUESTION: Who was Satanta?

Answer: Nomadic hunters who were known as the finest horsemen on the Plains

QUESTION: Who were the Comanche?

Oklahoma Prestigious Politics

☆ ☆ ☆ ☆ ☆ ☆ ☆ ☆ ☆ ☆ ☆ ☆ ☆ ☆ ☆ ☆ ☆

Answer: Number of counties in Oklahoma

QUESTION: What is 77?

Answer: Branch of state government that carries out the state's laws

QUESTION: What is the executive branch?

Answer: Branch of state government that makes the state's laws

QUESTION: What is the legislative branch?

Answer: The branch of state government that interprets the state's laws

QUESTION: What is the judicial branch?

Answer: Each of Oklahoma's counties is governed by this.

QUESTION: What is a board of commissioners?

Oklahoma

Lofty Leaders

Answer: He served as the first territorial governor of Oklahoma Territory from 1890–1891.

QUESTION: Who was George Steele?

Answer: Governor known for his sense of humor and his toughness during the Depression era

QUESTION: Who was William Henry "Alfalfa Bill" Murray?

Answer: Olympic gymnast and gold medalist who grew up in Edmond

QUESTION: Who is Shannon Miller?

Answer: They founded 25 all-black towns in the Indian Territory after the Civil War.

QUESTION: Who were former slaves?

Answer: He was one of the nation's seven original astronauts and the first to make two space flights that orbited the earth.

QUESTION: Who was Leroy Gordon Cooper, Jr.?

Oklahoma Statehood

Answer: November 16, 1907

QUESTION: When did Oklahoma become a state?

Answer: Oklahoma was admitted to the U.S. as this state.

QUESTION: What is 46th?

Answer: Charles N. Haskell

QUESTION: Who was the first governor of Oklahoma?

Answer: City that served as the first state capital

QUESTION: What is Guthrie?

Answer: The president who signed Oklahoma's official statehood proclamation

QUESTION: Who was Theodore Roosevelt?

Oklahoma
State Nicknames

Answer: Oklahoma's official state nickname

QUESTION: What is the "Sooner State"?

Answer: The nickname given people who sneaked into the Oklahoma territory to claim land before the official starting time of a land run

QUESTION: Who were "Sooners"?

Answer: Nickname that came from promoters who called Oklahoma the "promised land" in the 1880s

QUESTION: What is the "Boomer State"?

Answer: Oklahoma has more reservoirs than any other state; maybe that's where this nickname comes from.

QUESTION: What is "America's Frontier Lake State"?

Answer: Oklahoma's history could be the key to this nickname.

QUESTION: What is the "Land of Six Countries"?

Oklahoma Flag Facts

Answer: The first flag flown in Oklahoma in 1541 by Francisco Vasquez de Coronado

QUESTION: What was the Spanish flag?

Answer: After the Louisiana Purchase, this country's flag flew in Oklahoma.

QUESTION: What was the United States flag?

Answer: This country's flag, with a depiction of an ancient Aztec legend, flew over the Panhandle from 1821-1836.

QUESTION: What is Mexico?

Answer: A Native American tribe in southeastern Oklahoma who had their own government, codes of law, school system, and flag

QUESTION: Who were the Choctaw?

Answer: This flag with the buckskin shield of the Osage warrior on a blue background flies in the state today.

QUESTION: What is the Oklahoma state flag?

Oklahoma

Arts & Artists

Answer: World-renowned artists are featured at the OK Mozart Festival held here every year.

QUESTION: What is Bartlesville?

Answer: Osage dancer who was prima ballerina for the New York City Ballet for 13 years

QUESTION: Who was Maria Tallchief?

Answer: He is known for painting the four historically accurate murals in the dome of the state capitol building.

QUESTION: Who is Charles Banks Wilson?

Answer: His sculpture *As Long as the Waters Flow*, a tribute to the contributions made by Native Americans, stands in front of the capitol.

QUESTION: Who is Allan Houser?

Answer: He was a folksinger and composer best known for "This Land Is Your Land."

QUESTION: Who was Woody Guthrie?

Answer: The name given to the territory claimed by La Salle for France

QUESTION: What was Louisiana?

Answer: France gave the province of Louisiana to this country in 1762.

QUESTION: What is Spain?

Answer: In 1800, Spain gave Louisiana to them.

QUESTION: Who were the French?

Answer: The name given to the 1803 land purchase

QUESTION: What is the Louisiana Purchase?

Answer: Land located in the Indian Territory that was not assigned to any specific tribes

QUESTION: What were Unassigned Lands?

Oklahoma

Literary Laureates

Answer: Nationally syndicated newspaper columnist and humorist who grew up on a ranch in the Cherokee Nation

QUESTION: Who was Will Rogers?

Answer: Native American novelist who wrote the children's book *Circle of Wonder* and won a Pulitzer Prize for *House Made of Dawn*

QUESTION: Who is N. Scott Momaday?

Answer: Inducted into the Oklahoma Hall of Fame in 1978, he wrote several books on the history of blacks in America including *From Slavery to Freedom: A History of Negro Americans.*

QUESTION; Who was John Hope Franklin?

Answer: Popular mystery novelist who writes about the Navajo

QUESTION: Who is Tony Hillerman?

Answer: Novelist who is best known for *Invisible Man*, one of the first works to describe racial problems from an African-American point of view

QUESTION: Who is Ralph Ellison?

Oklahoma

Natural Resources

Answer: City born on the day of the 1889 Land Run that sits on one of the richest oil fields in the world

QUESTION: What is Oklahoma City?

Answer: City that became known as the “oil capital of the world” in the early 1900s

QUESTION: What is Tulsa?

Answer: Mineral discovered in Pittsburg County in the Choctaw Nation in the 1870s

QUESTION: What is coal?

Answer: Mineral mined in the north-central Great Salts Plain region

QUESTION: What is salt?

Answer: They provide the hardwood lumber used for building construction and furniture making.

QUESTION: What are forests?

Oklahoma

From A to Z

Answer: The state reptile

QUESTION: What is the Mountain Boomer Lizard?

Answer: The state rock

QUESTION: What is Barite Rose Rock?

Answer: The state tree

QUESTION: What is the Redbud?

Answer: The state wildflower

QUESTION: What is Indian Blanket?

Answer: The state monument

QUESTION: What is the *Golden Driller?*